THE DRU

Esoteric Wisdom of the Ancient Celtic Priests

selections from the work of

RUDOLF STEINER

Sophia Books

All translations revised by Christian von Arnim

Sophia Books
An imprint of Rudolf Steiner Press
Hillside House, The Square
Forest Row, East Sussex
RH18 5ES

www.rudolfsteinerpress.com

Published by Rudolf Steiner Press 2001

Series editor: Andrew Welburn
For earlier English publications of individual selections see p. 79

The material by Rudolf Steiner was originally published in German
in various volumes of the 'GA' (*Rudolf Steiner Gesamtausgabe* or
Collected Works) by Rudolf Steiner Verlag, Dornach. This
authorized volume is published by permission of the Rudolf Steiner
Nachlassverwaltung, Dornach (for further information see p. 83)

A catalogue record for this book is available from the British Library

ISBN 1 85584 099 5

Cover illustration by Anne Stockton. Cover design by
Andrew Morgan
Typeset by DP Photosetting, Aylesbury, Bucks.
Printed and bound in Great Britain by Cromwell Press Limited,
Trowbridge, Wilts.

Contents

Introduction: Esoteric Wisdom and the Spirit of the Ancient Celts

by Andrew J. Welburn

A well-known writer on the Druids (and other matters Celtic) recently prefaced his collection of essays on the subject with the comment that everything we actually know is contained in a few brief passages of Caesar's *Gallic Wars*; 'the rest,' as he engagingly put it, 'is speculation'.[1]

What Caesar tells us about the priesthood-intelligentsia of his arch-enemies in Britain and Gaul (France), moreover, is obviously highly selective, not to say biased. Writing a first-person account of his own ruthless campaign, and anxious to justify his violent suppression of their activities when sub-jugating their lands, he presents them to his Roman readers as barbarians who indulge in superstition and human sacrifices. Only a basic minimum of objective information can be assumed to underlie his statements to give plausi-bility to the whole. It is scarcely to be wondered at, therefore, that the speculation has been rife. It has been fuelled in turn by the nature of the evidence from the Celtic side; the ancient culture of which the Druids formed part was founded on oral tradition, rather than written texts, so that the literary sources on which later knowledge is based were often written many centuries after the original events. Much survives in the form of esoteric traditions, and imaginative myth and story. But how far can this restore to us the reality of the ancient world, or enable us to enter into the real stature and authority of these mysterious figures? The problem is to find a solid foothold. For instance, tradition links the Druids with the famous stone monuments or megaliths, of which Stonehenge forms one of the latest but best-known examples. A solid enough link to those ancient times, it might seem! But we know now through archaeology that these are actually much much older than the Celtic civilization to which the Druids belonged.[2] So even though we might be able to deduce many things about those who raised them, even perhaps concerning the spatial and cosmic meaning in their patterning of the stones, how are we to fathom what they might have meant to the Druid priests?

To help get us inside the living reality of Druidic spirituality, Rudolf Steiner invites us to take the opposite approach. First, from his point of view, we need to understand the inner side of the archaic experience of the world, the kind of consciousness which humanity brought to the matters of life, death and social renewal. The riddling fragments of our knowledge concerning the Druids might then fall into place.

Caesar describes on the one hand the esoteric, specialist nature of the Druids' knowledge ('they do not think it right to commit this teaching to writing ... and do not want their teaching spread abroad') and on the other, the congregating of the people, especially the young men, evidently to be initiated into their social roles as adults under the guidance of the priests.[3] This points to a time when all the knowledge belonging to society flowed from esoteric sources – that is to say, from a kind of consciousness which was not shared by everyone, but only those who had been through special processes. Caesar mentions several stages of initiation, and a training which could last over 20 years; and also that the Druids had the power to 'excommunicate' those they disapproved of. Alongside the Druids and closely related to them, Caesar mentions 'bards' and 'seers'. Thus as well as the legal-judicial, the cultural and artistic traditions were likewise intimately bound up with the Mysteries, as was the knowledge, we may suppose, of the seers relating to the gods, their relationship to nature, healing and agriculture.

The nature of the Mysteries, and the situation as Caesar found it in Britain and Gaul, looks back to a different *kind* of consciousness from that of our modern age. The 'knowledge of the oak' (the original meaning of 'Druid') belonged not to the kind of conceptual knowledge which can nowadays be made known through education, reading, etc., but to an 'imaginal' consciousness, as Steiner calls it – one that grasped things in imaginations. By this he is very far from meaning anything subjective, or merely pictorial. He uses the term technically to designate a kind of consciousness that does not stand outside the world, working out what it means, but which enters right into things; the images of things do not then 'stand for' some higher reality, but the higher reality is felt to be present in and informing them. He describes this from one point of view as a 'two-dimensional' consciousness, or plane-consciousness, because it shows us the world not as if we were looking on at three-dimensional 'objective' forms, but from a perspective where we are merged into the world, as if the third dimension had disappeared, and we could enter right into things. One might connect this kind of planar apprehension with those 'spiralling' forms which appear everywhere on the old Irish and related monuments, which lead us into the inner, two-dimensional reality where we are at one with what we perceive, as with a *mandala*, or the *nierika* of the shamans. Rudolf Steiner describes the way that, with this kind of consciousness, the old seers could discover the inner properties of natural forms, herbs or roots. Within the tiny outer, physical forms of the latter, for instance, they could experience 'giant' powers, undreamed of by those who could not awaken the imaginations through the training furnished by the Mysteries.[4]

Moreover, whereas our modern conceptual knowledge remains, except when we actually use it and bring it to life, an empty abstraction, or letters on a page, the imaginations experienced by the seers and Druids of ancient times when once awakened persisted as living sources of spiritual insight, which could be experienced again and again by those who approached them at the sacred site. In fact, in those archaic times it was absolutely necessary to go to such special localities in order to obtain knowledge, which could not be written down or transmitted abstractly; it had to be experienced anew by those who were able to go and train at the Mystery sites. For those who go through a related but rather different training today, it is still possible to experience something of these imaginations. Rudolf Steiner speaks in a particularly direct and moving way about what it meant to him to perceive them in the region of Penmaenmawr.[5] And the qualities they gave to the Conference there he regarded as especially valuable to the whole development of the spiritual-scientific approach, or 'anthroposophy', by which he believed that the modern world could rediscover the spiritual treasures of the past.[6]

It is by bringing to the question his insights into the imaginative and higher states of consciousness attained in the Mysteries, then, that Rudolf Steiner helps us to understand the world of the Druid priests. Many of the older scholarly attempts foundered because they were looking for something they called 'Druidism', i.e. a set of religious tenets, or ideas specific to this priestly class. Instead, we have to see the Druids as heirs to the old clairvoyant consciousness that lived in imaginations, which itself had been the common possession of humanity in times still further removed. These were what Rudolf Steiner called the 'pre-religious age', when the experience of the spiritual did not yet couch itself in thoughts, ideas and beliefs, but when it was a direct perception.[7] Subsequently, the development of individual thinking and the 'objective consciousness' we know today, emerging very gradually over centuries and indeed millennia of spiritual history, led to the disappearance or at least the overlaying of this archaic faculty. The Mysteries however kept the connection to it, and harmonized its use with the needs of the people under changing spiritual conditions. As scholars gave up the quest for a Druidic 'religion', they began to see that the Druids rather made sense against the backdrop of spiritual practices that reached back much further, and more widely — ultimately into the deep recesses of the Indo-European myths and the family of cultures that they had inspired, including the Germanic branch as well as the Celtic, and even connecting with ancient India and Iran. One scholar has noted, for instance, that the 'heathen' rites still enacted in medieval Ulster essentially reproduce the *aśvamedha* sacrifice of a horse known from the *Vedas*.[8] The veneration of the oak which gave the Druids their name is also a widespread Indo-European feature rather than a specifically Druidic or Celtic idea. In general, writes Stuart Piggott, 'inference from the archaeological evidence suggests ... a pattern of society going back in barbarian Europe to at least the middle of the second millennium BC.'[9] By looking back even further, to the third and fourth millennia,[10] Rudolf Steiner anticipates those experts who would now see the Celtic languages and culture growing gradually out of such older civilizations, rather than being brought to the West by sudden invasions. It is important to realize that he is not leading us away from the Druids' Mystery-knowledge but tracing it to its sources in the once much more widespread atavistic-clairvoyant consciousness of those prehistoric times.

In this way we can approach the issue of Druid use of the stone circles too. In the nature of things, there is no evidence at all of Druid involvement at these much earlier sites. But we may assume that they were still able to connect with a consciousness similar to that which first created them, and

make use of the cosmic and spiritual imaginations underlying them. It is also more than likely that in the distinctive
circular (or polygonal) temples of Romano-Celtic Britain we
have, as some archaeologists have surmised, a continuation
of 'native models' based on the older stone and wood
monuments. Rudolf Steiner was particularly struck by the
way that the ground-plan of these shrines and the older
megaliths coincided with that of his own great 'masterpiece
of sculptural architecture', the Goetheanum near Basel in
Switzerland.[11] Though certainly no Druid temple, the
extraordinarily creative forms of the building echo both the
natural landscape around, e.g. the distinctive morphology of
the hills, and the forms shaped by inner needs from within,
from the spiritual activities for which it provides a space. In a
freely creative, modern way, it too thus enables us to bring
spirit and nature back together again, rather as they were
once experienced in imaginations by those under the guidance of the Druid priests. It is yet another example of how
Rudolf Steiner's insights enable us at once to approach the
past with a living sense of the consciousness of those times,
and yet discover it out of our own experience and the
spiritual life of today. Such indeed is the basic principle of all
Mysteries.

The principle applies equally to the aspect of the Druidic
culture to which Steiner turns in the later lectures included in
this little book. Here he traces how Celtic Christianity con-
tinued the vision of the Mysteries in its special development
in Ireland (Hibernia). The deep affinity of Ireland to the
Christian message through that pre-Christian vision of the

initiates, and at the same time the elements of struggle between forces of the past and those of the future, are placed in a brilliant new light. It may not be too much to suggest that the best hope for resolving the profounder human issues in what Rudolf Steiner already called that 'troubled island' is to understand more deeply the reality behind the spiritual traditions there. To acknowledge the past while finding the openness to recreate it in new forms out of changing consciousness may be the way, as it once was for the Druid priests, to bring the harmony of shared spiritual goals into the troubled world we know today.

1. The Druids at Penmaenmawr

If we are to understand the message of the Druids, we need to have a sense for the way they experienced the world. In this introductory study and the one which follows, Rudolf Steiner takes us deeply into the ancient clairvoyant consciousness on which their wisdom was based. It is also a rare instance of his discussing his own personal experiences – obviously the spiritual atmosphere of Penmaenmawr possessed a very special potency! But throughout, a double perspective is in evidence. His approach is not based on going back to a long-lost age of spiritual vision. It is about how we can rediscover the sources of the ancient mystery-wisdom anew, with our modern freedom and scientific knowledge intact. It is only when we know how to find our own way to those sources, in fact, that we will be able to value the heritage of the Druids aright.

Recently I was invited by our English anthroposophical friends to give a course of lectures at Penmaenmawr.[12] Penmaenmawr is in Wales, where the island of Anglesey lies over against the west coast of Britain. It is really an extraordinary region which shows that the earth has many quite different geographies from those you will find discussed in textbooks, even for the most advanced students. Under normal circumstances, we think it more than enough if a geographical description includes the character of the vegetation, flora and fauna and if in addition it is based on the geological and palaeontological features of the region. But the earth displays differentiations of a much more inward nature than any you will normally find in a geographical work.

Thus in Penmaenmawr, where these lectures were held, you have only to go a short distance, a mile or so into the mountains, and all over the place you can find the remains of the old Druid cults, fallen stone circles of a simple sort. For instance, stones are put together to enclose a small space and covered with another stone so as to form a little chamber, where the light of the sun could be cut off, leaving the chamber in darkness. I do not dispute that such *cromlechs* also served as burial places, for at all times the most important centres of worship have been set up over the graves of fellow human beings. But here, even with these simple cromlechs, we have something in addition, as we can see from the so-called Druid circles.

It was a wonderful experience when I went with a friend one day to one of these mountains at Penmaenmawr, on which the few remains of two such circles are still to be seen lying very close to each other. Even today it can be seen from the position of the stones that there were once twelve of them, and if one wants to discover their purpose they must be observed closely. Now while the sun follows its course through the cosmos, whether during a day or during a year, a quite specific shadow is cast beneath each stone; and the path of the sun could be traced by following the shadow as it changed in the course of a day or year. We are still sensitive to light today, especially if light is associated with warmth or warmth with light.

With our consciousness today we naturally notice the difference between the light of the summer and winter sun, since we are warm in summer and cold in winter; and we may note finer differences too. But the same differences we notice so obviously in the light when we are either warm or freezing can be perceived in the shadow as well. There is a difference between the October sun and the July or August sun, not only in the direction but in the quality of the shadow it casts. One of the tasks of the Druids was to develop a special faculty for perceiving the quality of the shadow—for perceiving, for instance, the peculiar intermingling of a red tone in the August shadow or of a blue one in November or December.

Thus the Druids were able, by the training they received, to read off the daily and yearly course of the sun through its shadow. We can still see from these remains that one of the tasks they undertook was something of this sort. There were many other things that belonged to this religious ceremony, a sun ritual, which was not a mere abstraction, however, not even the abstraction we see in devotion and reverence. Without undervaluing devotion and reverence, it would be a complete error to believe that. Devotion and reverence were not in this case the essentials, for the religious ceremony, comprised something quite different.

Take grain of wheat or rye. It must be planted in the earth at a particular moment of the year, and it is not good if it is planted at the wrong time. Anyone who has exact knowledge of these things is well aware that it makes a difference whether a seed is planted a few days earlier or later. There are other things of this sort in human life. The people who lived about three thousand years ago in the region where the Druid cult flourished led an extremely simple life. Agriculture and cattle rearing were the chief occupations. But how did they know when to sow and harvest in the best way, or when to attend to the many other jobs which nature requires in the course of a year? Nowadays of course we have farmers' calendars which tell the farmer that on such and such a day such and such a job needs to be done, and tell him very intelligently. In our day, with our type of consciousness, this information can be catalogued and read off from the printed page. We think nothing of it, but the fact remains that there was none of that, not even the most primitive form of reading and writing, in the days when the Druid religion was in its prime. On the other hand, the Druids could stand in one of these stone circles and by observing the shadow they could make known, for instance, that during the next week farmers must undertake this or that work, or that the bulls be introduced to the herd since the moment was right for mating with the cows. The Druids were equipped to read in the cosmos; they used the signs produced by those monuments of which we have today only such few remains, and could read from them the information the sun gave them of what needed to be done on earth.

The constitution of the soul was in fact quite different, and it would be seriously arrogant on our part if, just because we are capable of this little bit of reading and writing, we were to undervalue the art which made it possible to specify the work and activities required on earth through these revelations of the heavens. In places like Penmaenmawr we are impelled to recollect many other things, too, which spiritual science is singularly qualified to investigate.

I have often pointed out in anthroposophical circles how ordinary thoughts are inadequate to grasp what spiritual science can investigate and how we have to conceive it in imaginations. I assume you all know what I have said about imaginations in my book *How to Know Higher Worlds*. It is these imaginations and not our ordinary ideas which we must have in our souls when we are describing things on the basis of some immediate spiritual observation and not of external sense perception.[13] The genuinely spiritual scientific accounts which you find in our anthroposophical lectures have their origin in imaginations of that kind.

Now these imaginations are much more alive than ordinary abstract thoughts, which can give us no inkling of what reality is, but only pictures of it. Imaginations, on the other hand, can be grasped by active thinking in the same way that we can grasp tables and chairs. We are much more vigorously permeated by reality when our knowledge comes from imaginations and not from abstract concepts. Anyone who speaks on the basis of imaginations always has them before him as though he were writing something down — though writing not with those terribly abstract signs which constitute our writing, but in cosmic pictures.

Now what is the position with regard to these imaginations in this region here?[14] Anyone who knows them knows also that it is pretty easy to attain them, pretty easy to form them. If people have a sense of responsibility when describing anything on the basis of spiritual science, they will allow these imaginations to take effect — that is, inscribe them in the spirit — only when they have thought about them a good deal and tested them thoroughly. Nobody who speaks with a full sense of responsibility on the basis of knowledge gathered in the spiritual world does so superficially. Nevertheless we can say that in regions such as this one it is relatively easy to inscribe these imaginations, but they are obliterated equally easily. If in regions like this we create spiritual content in imaginations — I cannot put it in any other way — we find it is like writing something down and immediately afterwards rubbing it out. But there in Wales, where land and sea meet and the tides ebb and flow each day, where the wind blows through and through you — for instance in the hotel where we were staying you not only felt the wind blowing in at the windows, but when one walked on the carpet it was like walking on a rough sea because of the wind blowing under the carpet — where nature is so full of life and so joyful in its life that you may get almost hourly alternations of rain and sunshine, then you really do come to see how nature revealed herself to the Druid priests (or I might say the learned Druids, for it would be the same thing) when they gazed upon nature from their mountain heights.

How, then, did the earth appear to the Druid's spiritual eye when the heavens had the character I have just described?

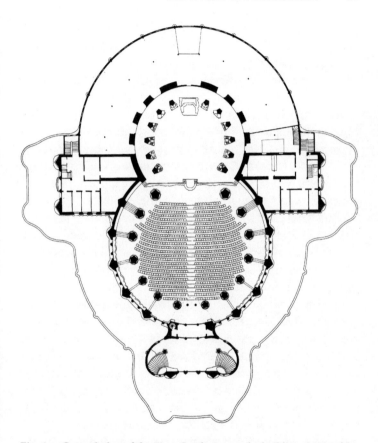

Fig. 1: Ground-plan of the First Goetheanum, the building designed by Rudolf Steiner as the centre for anthroposophy, on the Dornach hill near Basel in Switzerland. He noted how its plan resembles those of the Druid temples and stone circles, as may be seen in the examples shown (Figs. 2 and 3).

This is a very interesting question, though you will only comprehend it fully if you can understand the particular geographical quality of the place. In Wales you have to exert yourself much more vigorously if you want to construct imaginations than you do here for instance. There they are much more difficult to inscribe in the astral sphere. On the other hand they are more permanent and are not so easily erased. You come to realize how these old Druids chose for their most important religious centres specifically those locations in which the spiritual, as it approaches humankind, expresses itself to some extent in the quality of the place. Those Druid circles we visited — well, if we had gone up in a balloon and looked down from above on the larger and the smaller circles they would have appeared like the ground-plan of the Goetheanum which has been destroyed by fire.[15] It is a wonderfully situated spot!

As you climb the heights, you have wide views over land and sea. Then you reach the top and the Druid circles lie before you where the hill is hollowed out so that you find yourself in a ring of hills, and within this ring of hills are the Druid circles. It was there that the Druids sought their science, their knowledge, their wisdom; there that they sought their sun wisdom but also their nature wisdom. As the Druids penetrated into the relationship between what they saw on earth and what streamed down from the heavens, they saw the whole processes of plant growth and vegetation quite differently from the way in which they appear to our abstract thought of later days. If we can properly grasp the true quality of the sun, on the one hand

the physical rays which enter our eyes, on the other the
shadow with its various gradations, we come to realize that
the spiritual essence of the sun lives on in the various grades
of shadow. The shadow prevents only the physical rays of
the sun from reaching other bodies, whereas the spiritual
penetrates further.

In the *cromlechs* which I have described to you, a small
dark place is separated off. But it is only the physical sunlight
which cannot penetrate there, the sun's activity does penetrate. The Druids gained access to the secrets of the world as
gradually through this activity they came to be permeated by
the secret forces of cosmic existence. Thus, for instance, the
action of the sun on plants was revealed to them; they could
see that a particular kind of plant life flourishes at a particular time when the sun is active in a particular way. They
could trace the spiritual activity of the sun and see how it
pours and streams into flowers, leaves and roots; and it was
the same with animals.

And while they were thus able inwardly to recognize the
activity of the sun, they also began to see how other activities
from the cosmos, those of the moon for instance, pour into
the earth. They could see that the effect of the sun was to
promote upwards sprouting growth, and so they knew that
if a plant as it grows out from the soil were exposed only to
the sun, it would never stop growing. The sun produces
burgeoning, luxuriant life. If this life is checked and reduced
to a specific form, if leaves, blossoms, seeds and fruit assume
a specific shape, if what strives towards the infinite is vari-
ously limited — all this has its origin in the activities of the

moon. And such activity is to be found not only in the reflected light of the sun, for the moon reflects all influences; these in their turn can be seen in the growth of the plant out of its root and in what lives in the propagation of animals and much else.

Let us take a particular instance. The Druids observed the growing plant; they observed in a more living way what, later on, Goethe observed more abstractly in his idea of metamorphosis. The Druids saw the downward streaming sun forces, but they saw also the reflected sun forces in everything that gives the plant its form. In their natural science they saw the combined activity of sun and moon in every single plant and animal. They could perceive the action of sun and moon on the root which is wholly within the earth and has the function of absorbing the salts of the earth in a particular way. They could see that the action of sun and moon was quite different on the leaf, which wrests itself out of the earth and presses forward into the air. Again, they saw a different action on the flower, which pushes onwards to the light of the sun. They could see as a unity the activity of the sun and moon, mediated by the activity of the earth. To them, plant growth and the being of the animal were also a unity.

Of course the Druids' life there was just what we experienced with the raging winds, revealing so much about the structure of the region with the particular weather conditions which manifest themselves so vividly there. Thus, for example, at the beginning of one of our eurythmy performances, which took place in a wooden hall, the audience

sat with their umbrellas up because just before the performance there had been a heavy downpour which was still
going on when the performance began. The curtains were
quite wet![16] This intimate association with nature which can
still be experienced today was of course also experienced by
the Druids. Nature there is not so hard; it almost embraces
one. It really is a delightful experience. I might almost say
that one is drawn on and accompanied by the activity of
nature; one seems to be part of it. I even met people who
maintained that one need not really eat there, that one can be
fed by this very activity of nature!

The Druids, then, lived with their sun initiation within this
activity of nature and saw as the unity I have described the
sun and moon mediated through the activity of the earth, the
growth of the plant, the growth of root, leaf and flower; and
all this not in the form of abstract laws as today, but of living
elemental beings. Different elemental beings of sun and
moon were active in the root, in the leaf and in the flower.
They could also pursue in the wider realms of nature what is
so beneficially differentiated in root, leaf and flower.
Through their imaginative gifts, they could see the small
elemental beings restricted to narrow limits in the root, and
they knew that what lives in beneficial form in the root can
free itself and expand to become huge. Thus they saw the
large-scale activities of nature as the small activities of the
plant raised to gigantic proportions. Just as they spoke about
the elemental beings in the root of the plant, they could also
refer to these root beings as having grown in a cosmically
irregular way to manifest in the formation of frost, dew and

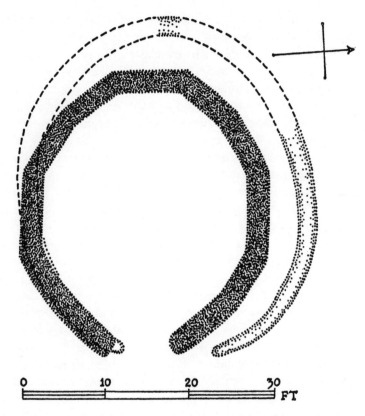

Fig. 2:   Ground-plan of Romano-Celtic temple excavated at Brigstock, Northants.

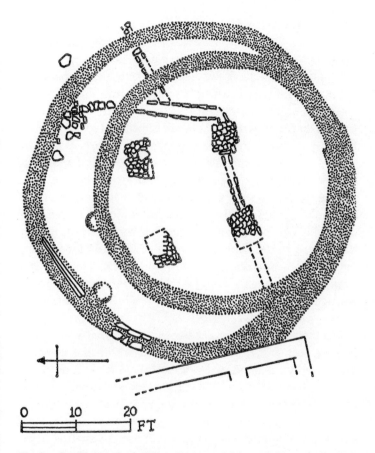

Fig. 3:   Double circular building, Romano-Celtic, probably a temple. Note the four column bases in the inner circle structure. Winterton, Lincs.

hail. On the one hand they spoke of the root beings who were beneficially active, and of the giants of frost and ice who were these root beings grown to gigantic size.

Again, they spoke of the elemental activities in the leaf of the plant, which are permeated with the forces of the air; they traced them into the distant spaces of nature, and then saw that if what lives in the leaf liberates itself and strives beyond its proper limits into the expanses of nature, it will be manifest in the surging winds. The giants of wind and storm are the elemental beings of the plant grown beyond their size. And the element which is distilled in the flower and meets the sunlight and produces in the flower the ethereal oils with their phosphoric quality — if that is freed, it manifests itself as the giants of fire, to whom Loki for instance belongs.[17] In this science of sun and moon, therefore, the Druids saw as a unity both that which lives in the narrowly restricted space of the plant and that which frees itself and lives in wind and weather.

But they went further. They said: when that which lives in root, leaf and flower is contained within the desirable limits set by the good gods, normal plant growth results. If it appears in hoar frost, that is the work of opposing beings; for the elemental beings, growing into powers of opposition, create the harmful, devastating aspects of nature. Now as a human being I can make use of the devastating activities of the beings who are the opponents of the gods; I can gather the hoar frost in appropriate ways, and the products of the storm and whatever is caught up in the surging of wind and rain. I can make use of the giant forces for my own purposes by burning the plant, for instance, and reducing it to ashes, to charcoal and so on. I can take these forces, and by using frost, hail and rain and other such things, or what the giants of fire control—things which are the expression of forces that have grown to harmful vastness—I can protect the normal growth of the plant. I can rob these giants of all forces and can treat normal plants with them, and by applying these forces of the opposing powers I can make healing medicines out of the good elemental forces which have remained within their proper limits. And this was in fact one of the ways of making medicines out of plants, by employing frost and snow and ice and by the use of burning and calcination. The Druids felt it to be their work to take whatever was harmful from the opposing giant powers and restore it to the service of the good gods. We can trace these things in many different ways.

Now why am I spending time on this? I want to use it as an example—and I quote this particular one because I do indeed think that the Penmaenmawr lecture course was a very important event in the history of the anthroposophical movement[18]—to show how the consciousness of human beings and their whole constitution of soul were quite different at a time not so very far removed from the present. With their present-day consciousness, human beings cannot realize what lived in the consciousness of this ancient humanity. And what I have said of that ancient humanity could also be said of other peoples. There we catch glimpses of a quite different constitution of soul. People in those days had no idea of what we experience as abstract thoughts. All their thinking was more dreamlike, and they did not live within such sharply outlined ideas and concepts as we do today. They lived in dreams which were much more vivid and alive, more full of substance; and indeed their waking life was really a sort of continuation of their dreaming. Just as nowadays we live in an alternation of dreaming or dreamless sleep and the abstract ideas of our waking life, so they alternated between this dreamlike everyday life and a dreamless sleep that was not wholly like ours. When they woke they felt that there was still something remaining over from sleep—something which afforded a sort of nourishment for the soul, which they had absorbed during sleep and which could still be felt, indeed, could still be 'tasted'. In those days human beings felt the after-taste of sleep in their whole organism. There was a third condition which no longer occurs in human consciousness, a feeling of being surrounded by the earth, and when a person woke up he felt not only that he had been asleep—of which he retained an after-taste—but that he had been received into a kind of grave by the forces of gravity, that gravity had closed him in and he was in what might be described as the embrace of the earth. Now just as we can describe our present-day states of consciousness as waking, dreaming and sleeping, so we should have to say that at a certain stage of the past there were the three states of dreaming, sleeping and being embraced by the earth.

Excursus: Spiritual imaginations

Let us once more call up before our souls where modern initiation leads after the first steps to imaginative knowledge have been successfully taken. Human beings then come to the point where their previous abstract, purely ideational world of thought is permeated with inner life. The thoughts coming to them are no longer lifeless and passively acquired; they are an inward world of living force which they feel in the same way as they feel the pulsing of their blood or the streaming in and out of the air they breathe. It is therefore a question of the ideational element in thinking being replaced by an inward experience of reality. Then the pictures that previously constituted a person's thoughts are no longer mere abstract, shadowy projections of the outside world, but are teeming with an inward, vivid existence. They are real imaginations experienced in two dimensions.

However, it is not the same as a person standing in front of a painting in the physical world, for that would be like a vision, not an imagination. It is rather as though, having lost the third dimension, the person were himself moving about within the picture. It is therefore not like seeing something in the physical world; anything that has the look of the physical world is a vision. Genuine imagination comes to us only when, for example, we no longer see colours as we do in the physical world, but when we experience them. What does this mean? When you see colours in the physical world, they give you different experiences. You perceive red as something that attacks you, that wants to spring at you. A bull will react violently to this aggressive red; it experiences it far more vividly than do human beings, in whom the whole experience is toned down. When you perceive green, it gives you a feeling of balance, an experience neither painful nor particularly pleasant; whereas blue induces a mood of devotion and humility.

If we allow these various experiences of colour to penetrate right into us, we can realize how it is that when anything in the spiritual world comes at us in the aggressive way that red does in physical life it is something corresponding to the colour red. When we encounter something which calls up a mood of humility, this has the same effect as the experience of blue or blue-violet in the physical world. We can simplify this by saying: we have experienced red or blue in the spiritual world. Otherwise, for the sake of precision, we should always have to say: we have experienced something there in the way that red, or blue, is experienced in the physical world. To avoid so many words, one says simply that one has seen auric colours which can be distinguished as red, blue, green, and so on.

2. The Sun Initiation of the Druid Priests and their Moon Science

We have been able to penetrate to some extent into Druid culture. With the means available today to external science, people will ask in vain as to what was the real soul constitution of these Druid priests. (I might just as well call them Druid sages, for both are expressions entirely suited to that age, although of course the terms did not exist then.) What was it that lived in the impulses by means of which these Druid priests guided their people?

What we are often told as history, and what indeed often sounds terrible, always refers to events which happened when an epoch was slipping into decadence and degeneration. What I am going to describe here always refers to what preceded such an epoch of degeneration and was active when the civilization was at its height. For these *cromlechs*, these sun circles, refer in their true meaning to what existed in the epoch when the Druid mysteries were in their prime. And with the methods given us by anthroposophical spiritual science we can in a certain way even today penetrate into the whole manner and mode of working of these Druid priests. It may be said that they were everything to their people, or rather their tribe. They were the authorities for the religious requirements, in so far as one can speak of religious requirements at that time. They were the authorities for the social impulses, and also for the healing methods of that time. They united in one all that later on was distributed over many branches of human civilization.

We obtain the right perspective on Druid culture — and it is quite correct to use this expression — only when we realize that its essence is to be found in an epoch preceding that which echoes to us from the mythological ideas of the North that are connected with the name of Wotan or Odin.[19] What is associated with the name of Wotan really lies later in time than this epoch when Druid culture was in its prime. In the orbit of wisdom that points to the divine name of Wotan or Odin, we must recognize something that comes over from the East, proceeding initially from Mysteries in the proximity of the Black Sea. The spiritual content of these Mysteries flowed from the East towards the West, in that certain 'colonizing' Mysteries, coming from the Black Sea and proceeding westwards, were founded in a variety of ways.

All this, however, streamed into a culture that must be called elevated in a deeper sense into a primordial wisdom, Druid wisdom. This Druid wisdom was really an unconscious echo, a kind of unconscious memory of the sun and moon elements existing on earth before the sun and moon were separated from it.[20] Initiation in the Druid mysteries was essentially a sun initiation bound up with what was then able to become moon wisdom through the sun initiation.

What was the purpose of these *cromlechs*, these Druid circles? They were there essentially for the purpose of a spiritual observation of the relationship of the earth to the sun. When we look at the single dolmens, we find that they are really instruments by which the outer physical effects of the sun were shut off in order that the initiate who was gifted with seership could observe the effects of the sun in a dark space. The inner qualities of the sun element, how these permeate the earth and how they are again radiated back from the earth into cosmic space—this was what the Druid priest was able to observe in the single *cromlechs*. The physical nature of the sunlight was shut out; a dark space was created by means of the stones fitted into the soil with a roof stone above them. In this dark space it was possible by the power of seeing through the stones to observe the spiritual nature and being of the sun's light.

Thus the Druid priest, standing before his altar, was concerned with the inner qualities of the sun element to the extent that he needed the wisdom that then streamed into him—streamed in such that the wisdom still had the character of a force of nature—for the purpose of directing and guiding his people. But we must always bear in mind that we are here speaking of an age when human beings could not look at the calendar to see when it was right to sow, when this or that seed ought to be put into the soil. In those ages human beings did not look at books in order to get information about the time of the year. The only book in existence was the cosmos itself. And the letters that formed themselves into words arose from the observations of how the sun worked on one or other contrivance that had been erected. Today, when you want to know something, you read. The Druid priest looked at the action of the sun in his *cromlech*, and there he read the mysteries of the cosmos. He read there when corn, rye, and so on were to be sown.

These are only examples. The impulses for all that was done were read from the cosmos. The greater impulses which were needed to complete the calendar were obtained from observation within the shadow of the Druid circle. So that in this age, when there was nothing that was derived from the human intellect, the cosmos alone was there. And instead of the printing-press, human beings had the *cromlech* in order to unravel from out of the cosmos the mysteries it contained.

Reading the cosmic book in this way, human beings were therefore concerned with the element of the sun. And in distinction to the sun element they perceived the moon element. The forces which were then concentrated in the moon were once united with the earth. These forces, however, did not wholly withdraw; they left something behind in the earth. If there had been sun forces alone, only rampantly growing cells would have been created, life elements always with the character of small or large cells. Diversity, the forming element, does not emanate from the sun forces but from the moon forces working together with the sun forces. When human beings exposed themselves to all that their circles, their *cromlechs* could reveal to them, the Druid priests did not receive the mere abstract impression which we today receive, quite rightly, when in our way — that is to say, in an intellectual way — we enter into the things of the spirit. For the forces of the sun spoke to them directly. In the shadow of the sun the spiritual nature of the sun worked into them

directly, and it worked far more intensely than a sense
impression does on us today for it was related to far deeper
forces. As the priest stood before his place of ritual, observing the nature of the sun, his breathing changed even as he
observed. It became lifeless, it was blunted, it went in waves
so that the one breath merged into the other. He, with all that
he was as a human being through his breath, lived in the
influence of the sun. And the outcome was not abstract
knowledge of some kind, but something that worked in him
like the circulation of the blood, pulsating inwardly through
him, kindling the human part of his being down to the
physical level. Yet this penetration of the physical was
spiritual at the same time, and the inner stimulation he
experienced was really his knowledge.

We must think of this knowledge in a very living way, as a
very intense, living experience. Moreover, the Druid priest
received it at certain times only. At a lesser intensity, it could
be brought to life in him every day at noon. But if the great
secrets were to be revealed, the priest had to expose himself
to these influences at the time which we now call the season
of St John. Then there arose what might be called the great
wave of his knowledge as against the lesser daily waves.
And as through the sun influences, which he thus captured
on earth in a particular and artificial way, he experienced
what he felt as his initiation—his sun initiation—he became
able also to understand the forces that had remained behind
as moon forces in the earth when the moon had left it. Those
were the laws of nature which he learned about under the
influence of sun initiation. What was revealed on the surface

of things was unimportant to him, but what welled up from below as the moon forces in the earth was important. Through the principle of initiation, whose relics are preserved in these strange monuments today, he placed himself in a state to receive knowledge. And the knowledge he gained was of all that works in nature, especially when in the sky at night-time the stars stood over the earth, and the moon travelled across the heavens.

Sun initiation gave the Druid priest the spiritual impulses that provided him with his science of nature. Our science of nature is an earth science. His was a moon science. He felt the underlying moon forces as they ray forth in the plants from the depths of earth, as they work in wind and weather and so forth. He felt the forces of nature not in the abstract way that we do today with our earth science. He felt them in all their living characteristics.

And what was thus livingly revealed to him he experienced as the elemental beings living in the plants, in the stones, in all things. These elemental beings, having their dwellings in trees and plants and so forth, were enclosed in certain bounds. But they were not those narrow bounds that are set for human beings today. They were far wider. His science of nature being a moon science, the Druid priest perceived how the elemental beings can grow and expand into gigantic size. This is where his knowledge of the Jötuns, the giant beings, came from.[21] When he looked into the roots of a plant beneath the soil, where the moon forces were living, he found the elemental being in its true bounds. But these beings were always endeavouring to grow outwards,

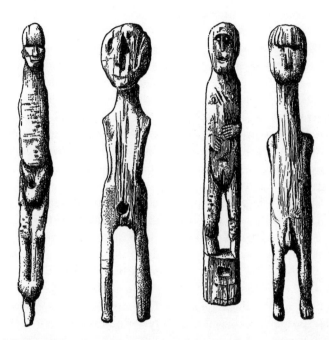

Fig. 4:   Celtic wood-carvings of spirits, nature-beings or similar entities. Classical authors say that such representations were 'everywhere' in Celtic sacred enclosures.

gigantically. When the kind of elemental beings who lived beneficially in the roots expanded into giants, they became the giants of the frost whose outward symbol is the frost and who live in all that sweeps over the earth as the destructive hoar frost and the other severe forces that are characterized by frost. The loosened root forces of the plants worked destructively when they lived within the frost as it swept with its giant forces over the earth, whereas in the root the same forces worked productively and beneficially. And what worked in the growth of the leaves too could grow to giant size. Then it lived as a giant elemental being in the murky storms that swept over the earth with all that they contained in certain seasons – the pollen of the plants, and so forth. And what lives gently, modestly, one might say, in the flower forces of the plants becomes all-destroying fire when it grows to giant size.

Thus in the weather processes the Druid priests saw the forces of beings expanded to giant size – the same forces that lived within their right limits in the kingdoms of nature. The chosen places where we find these old heathen centres of ritual show that what they received through the sun circles and the *cromlechs* was developed into earth knowledge. That is how such knowledge arose. They developed it so as to be able properly to observe the mysterious workings of wind and weather as they swept over the earth – the working together of water and air, the hoar frost oozing forth from the earth, the melting dew. It was through sun initiation and the knowledge of the moon beings that there arose this most ancient conception which we find at the very foundations of European culture.

Thus the Druid priest read and deciphered the cosmic secrets which his institutions of the sun initiation enabled him to gain from the cosmos. Stimulated by the sun initiation, he thus gained his knowledge from his science of moon-related nature. All of social and religious life was closely related to this. Everything which the priest told the people was based on the spiritual foundations of this element in which they lived. We see it best of all in what the Druid priests possessed as a science of healing. They saw on the one hand the elemental beings contained within their bounds in the various growths and products of the mineral and especially of the plant kingdom. Then they observed what happened to the plants when these were exposed to frost, exposed to the influences which the giants of the storm and wind carry through the airy spaces, or exposed to the seething fire-giants. They studied what the giants of frost and hoar frosts, the giants of the storm, the fire-giants would do to plants if released and set free. At length they came to the point of taking the plants themselves, and imitating within certain limits all that was indicated in outer nature as the influence of the giants. They subjected the plants to certain processes, to the freezing process, the process of burning, the process of binding and solution. The Druid priests said to themselves: 'Observing this world of nature, we see the destructive working of the giants, of frost and storm and fire. But we can take from these giants, from the Jötuns, what they spread so awkwardly and clumsily over the world; we can wrest it from them; we can harness once more within narrow limits these liberated forces of the moon.'

This they did. They studied what takes place in the thawing earth, in storm and wind, in the fierce, seething heat of the sun. All this they applied to the sun characteristics which lived in the plants and which they themselves received in their initiation. And in so doing they created their remedies, their healing herbs and the like, all of which were based upon the fact that the giants were reconciled with the gods. In those times each single remedy bore witness to the reconciliation of the opponents of the gods with the gods themselves.

What human beings received under the direct influences of sun and moon in the form offered by nature itself was food. A medicine, on the other hand, would be something that human beings themselves created by continuing nature beyond itself, harnessing the giant force to place it in the service of the sun.

We must imagine Druid civilization spread out over a great part of northern and central Europe about 3,000 or 3,500 years ago. There was nothing remotely similar to writing. There was only the cosmic script. Then this was infused from the East—to begin with from a Mystery centre in the region of the Black Sea—with what ordinary consciousness now considers as an insoluble riddle of Norse mythology associated with the name of Wotan. For what is Wotan? The Mystery from which the Wotan culture proceeded was a Mercury Mystery, a Mystery that supplemented the impulses of sun and moon with the impulse of Mercury. We might say that that old civilization existed in the innocence and simplicity radiated by sun and moon, untouched by what was imparted to human beings through the Jupiter impulses. Only away in the East these Jupiter impulses were already present. From there they now spread in a colonizing influence towards the West. Wotan-Mercury carried his influence westwards.

This also throws light upon the fact that Wotan is described as the bringer of runes, of the runic art of writing. He was the bringer of what human beings expressed at a basic primitive level of intellectual thinking as a way of deciphering the universe. The Wotan impulse is the very first appearance of intellectual thinking. Thus one might say that the character of Mercury, of Wotan, was now added to the characters of sun and moon.

Wherever the Wotan impulse came fully to expression, it influenced everything that was present from earlier experiences. Everything received a certain impulse from the Wotan element. For Druid culture has a special secret. We know that everywhere things arise that do not belong there, just like weeds grow on cultivated land. We might say that Druid culture only recognized the sun and moon qualities as the good plants of civilization, and if, leaping forward as it were to a later time, the intellectual element began at that time already, they treated it as a weed.

Among the many remedies the Druids had, there was one against the Mercury quality of deep thought and introspection. Strange as it may seem to us today, they had a remedy against this habit of sinking into one's inner being, or, as we say, of reflecting on one's own salvation. The Druids wanted human beings to live with nature and not to sink into themselves, and they regarded as sick and ill anyone who even attempted to express anything in symbols or the like unless it was merely to imitate the things of nature in a primitive form of art. Anyone who made symbols was diseased and had to be healed. Yes, my dear friends, if we with all our present knowledge were transposed into Druid culture, we should all be sent to hospital to be cured.

And now the Wotan civilization brought this very illness from the East. The Wotan civilization was indeed felt as an illness. But with a power grown truly great and gigantic, it also brought what had formerly appeared as an abnormality, an unhealthy introspection. Into the midst of what had formerly been taken only from the cosmic script, it introduced the rune. So that human beings now transferred their intellectual element into the symbols they made. The Wotan civilization introduced everything that was experienced as Mercury culture. Thus it is no surprise that what proceeded from the Wotan culture — distilled from the best forces it contained, namely, the being of Baldur, the sun being — was perceived as something not linked with life but with death. Baldur had to go to Hel, into the dark forces of death, the dwelling-place of death.[22] Moreover, as we can see from the traditions of the *Edda*, human beings to begin with reflected most not on the question of how Baldur, son of the Wotan forces, should be freed from Hel — for this is really a later idea — but on the question of how he should be healed. And finally they said: we have many means of healing, but for Baldur, the intelligence proceeding from the runes of Wotan, there are no remedies and it can only lead to death.

Thus we see once more what I have described from so many different aspects in the study of human evolution. In ancient times, human beings in their instinctive knowledge knew nothing of the significance of death; human beings remembered their pre-earthly life and knew that death is only a transformation. They did not feel death as an incision any deeper than this. Above all, there was no such thing as the tragedy of death.

This only entered with the Mystery of Golgotha, which became, indeed, redemption from the fear of death. In the Baldur legend, one can see most clearly how, with the entry of the intellectual element, there arises that mood of soul which expects death; and one can see what thus entered into human evolution. What was therefore experienced with the death of Baldur, who could not rise again, was only healed again in soul and spirit when the figure of Christ, who could rise from death, was set against that.

It is wonderful how an understanding of the Christ impulse was prepared in the North through the influence of the Mercury forces on the sun and moon forces. In Baldur, the god who falls into death and cannot rise again, we see the forerunner in the North of Christ, who also falls victim to death but who can rise again because he comes directly from the sun. Baldur, on the other hand, the sun force coming from Wotan, is the sun force reflected back by Mercury, shining out from the symbols which human beings create with their intellect.

Thus we see how all these things evolved in the northern regions, where human beings lived in and read the script of the cosmos, seeking their religious, social and medical ideas in the cosmos, until at a later stage they passed over to live with the earth forces. From his stone of sacrifice, the Druid priest observed the configuration of the shadow of the sun and read what appeared in the shadow, representing the spiritual aspect of the sun. Then we approach the time when the sun being that had been caught up, we might say, in the *cromlechs* is drawn in abstract lines called rays. We approach the time when the relationship of what lives in root and leaf and blossom with what lives in frost and wind and fire is recognized at most in a chemical sense. Both giants and elemental beings are transformed into 'forces of nature'. And yet our forces of nature are no more than the giants of ancient times. Only, we are not aware of the fact and feel immensely superior. It is a straight line of development from the giants to the forces of nature. These are their latter-day children. Human beings, who today live in a highly artificial — that is, an unoriginal — civilization, cannot but be deeply moved when they look at these scant relics of the Druid age. It is like seeing the ancient ancestors of our present time.

3. The Mysteries of Ancient Ireland (Hibernia)

The presence of the Celts in Britain and Ireland is now thought to go back much further than was previously supposed; also it was in Ireland above all that the Celtic spiritual heritage lived on into later centuries. Small wonder that Rudolf Steiner found rooted there the Mysteries which lay at the heart of the ancient spiritual wisdom. In their holy places, the Druid priests of ancient Ireland – 'Hibernia' – were able to deepen their experience of nature and the changing seasons into an awareness of spiritual-creative powers. The practices of the Mysteries which he describes are also the key to finding our own modern relationship to the realities behind these experiences, which are still accessible to the consciousness of today.

Today I propose to speak to you about the Mysteries once centred on the troubled island of Ireland, the Mysteries of Hibernia, to which I also refer in my Mystery Plays.[23]

Comparatively speaking, it is much more difficult to approach these ancient Hibernian Mysteries in what I have called in many of my writings the Akashic Record than it is in other cases, much more difficult for subsequent seers to find in that eternal record the images remaining there of these Mysteries than it is to find those of other Mystery centres. For in trying to approach the Hibernian Mysteries, the impression arises that the images contain extraordinarily powerful forces that repel one and thrust one back. Even if the images are approached with certain courage of vision — a courage which in other cases meets with less resistance than is experienced here — the opposition is so intense that it even gives rise to a kind of numbness. Knowledge of what I am about to describe to you is therefore fraught with obstacles, and in the next few days you will see why this is so.

In the Hibernian Mysteries, too, of course, there were initiates who had preserved much of the ancient wisdom of humanity and who, stimulated and inspired by this wisdom, were able to achieve a degree of seership themselves. There were also pupils, candidates for initiation, who by the special methods applied there were to be prepared to approach the secrets of the cosmic Word. The preparation given to those who were to be initiated in Hibernia was twofold. Firstly, all the difficulties involved in the acquisition of knowledge were brought home to the pupils; they were made inwardly aware of everything that can be a torment on the path to the kind of knowledge which does not yet penetrate into the depths of existence but which consists of exerting to the greatest possible extent all the powers of the soul belonging to everyday consciousness.

These pupils had to experience in their souls all the difficulties occurring on the path of knowledge of ordinary consciousness. They were compelled to endure every doubt, every torment, every inner struggle with its frequent dead-ends and deceptive leads for all the excellence of logic or dialectic — and then to experience the difficulties which make themselves felt when one has actually attained knowledge and wishes to bring it to expression. We can see that there are two aspects here: the struggle to attain a truth and then to bring it to expression, formulate it in words. Indeed, when the path of knowledge has been earnestly followed, there is always the feeling that what can be compressed into words is something which is no longer absolute truth, something which surrounds the truth with all kinds of stumbling blocks and pitfalls.

The pupils were made acquainted with the experience undergone by someone who has valiantly and genuinely struggled to attain knowledge.

Secondly, the pupils were led to experience in their soul life how little the knowledge acquired on the ordinary path of consciousness can, in the last resort, contribute to human happiness, how little human happiness can be promoted by dialectic or rhetoric. On the other hand, it was also made clear to the pupil that if he wanted to keep his bearings in life as a human being, he would have to involve himself with those things which can to a certain extent bring him joy and happiness. Thus they were driven to the verge of an abyss in two directions and always made to wonder whether they should wait until they were supplied with a bridge to cross each one. And they were so deeply initiated into the doubts and difficulties connected with the attainment of knowledge that when at last they were led from these preparatory stages to the actual approach to the cosmic secrets, they came to the decision that, if it had to be, they would even renounce knowledge; they would deny themselves everything that cannot make a person happy.

In these ancient Mysteries, the pupils were subjected to such severe tests that they came to the point where in the most natural and elementary way they developed feelings which ordinary, narrow reason regards as without foundation. It is easy to say that nobody would wish to forgo knowledge; that it goes without saying that one wants to gain knowledge, however great the difficulties might be. That, of course, is the attitude of people who do not know what the difficulties are, and who have not been deliberately led to experience them, as was the case with the pupils in the Mysteries of Hibernia. On the other hand, it is also easy to say that one will deny oneself both inner and outer happiness and tread a path of knowledge only. But to someone who knows the truth of these things, both declarations, so often made, appear utterly superficial. When the pupils had been prepared to the degree indicated, they were brought before two gigantic statues, enormous and majestic. One of them was majestic by reason of its external, spatial dimensions, while the other, of equal size, was impressive because of its special character. One statue was a male figure, the other female. By means of these two statues the pupils were to experience the approach of the cosmic Word. In a way they were the external letters with which the pupils were to begin to decipher the cosmic secret facing humanity.

The one statue, the male one, was of a thoroughly elastic material. Any part of it could be indented by pressure. And the pupils were told to push it in all over. This showed it to be hollow inside. It was really only the 'skin' of a statue but made of a thoroughly elastic material so that, when a pupil pressed it, it returned immediately to its original form. [...]

The effect of both statues together was intended to continue working in the subsequent soul life of the pupil as a combined impression. But the pupil was nevertheless now urged to let the impression from the male statue reverberate very powerfully within him. I will now describe to you the way this impression reverberated, but words have to be used, of course, that are not really suitable for representing an initiation experience, and the inner meaning of some of the things I say will have to be felt intuitively.

What the pupil experienced when he gave himself up to the impression of the male statue was a kind of soul rigidity, a rigid numbness of the soul which set in with greater and greater intensity the more he was told to let the echo persist; it was a soul rigidity which felt also like a bodily rigidity. In the intervening periods, the pupil was able to attend to all the necessities of life, but time and again his soul was transported back to this echo and he again experienced such rigidity. This was a type of initiation which was very strongly, even if not totally, reminiscent of the old style of the original Mysteries — and now this rigidity caused a change in the pupil's consciousness. One could not say that the consciousness was in any way dulled, but the pupil had the feeling that the state of consciousness in which he found himself was totally unfamiliar to him and that he could not handle it, did not know how to deal with it. As a consequence, all that the pupil felt was that his whole consciousness was entirely filled with the sensation of rigidity. At that point it was as though the pupil felt that what was rigid in him, namely, he himself, was being taken up into the cosmos. He felt as if he were being transported into the far spaces of the cosmos. And he could say to himself: 'The cosmos is receiving me.'

Then something very special happened. His consciousness was not extinguished but it became somewhat different. When this experience of numbness and of being received by the cosmos had lasted for a sufficient length of time — and this was ensured by the guides of the initiation — the pupil said something like this to himself: 'The rays of the sun and the stars are drawing me out into the cosmos, but nevertheless I remain within myself.' When this experience had lasted long enough, a remarkable vista presented itself. For the first time the pupil realized the purpose of this state of consciousness which had set in during the numbness, for now, due to his experiences and their echoes, there came to him all manner of impressions of winter landscapes. Winter landscapes were there in the spirit before him, landscapes in which he saw whirling snowflakes filling the air or landscapes in which he looked at things such as forests with snow weighing down the branches of the trees, things which absolutely reminded him of what he had seen in his everyday life but which always gave the impression of reality. So that after being transported into the cosmos he felt as though his own consciousness was conjuring up before him whole excursions in time through winter landscapes.

And during this experience he felt as if he were not actually in his body, but certainly in his sense organs; he felt that he was living with the whole of his being in his eyes, his ears and also on the surface of his skin. And then, when his whole sense of feeling and touch seemed to be spread out over his skin, he also felt as if he had become like the statue that is elastic but hollow. And he felt, for instance, that his eyes had an inner connection with these landscapes. He felt as though this whole landscape he was looking at was active in each eye, as though the eye were an inner mirror reflecting everything outside him.

Furthermore, he did not feel himself as a unity but felt his ego multiplied to the number of his senses, namely, twelvefold.[24] And on the basis of the feeling that his ego had become twelvefold, he had the remarkable experience that there was an ego which looked through his eyes, an ego which worked in his sense of thought, sense of speech, sense of touch, sense of life. It made him feel as if he were scattered over the world. This experience created an intense longing for union with the essence of the hierarchy of the angeloi in order that from this union strength and power might be acquired for mastering the split of the ego into the single sense experiences.[25] And all of this raised the question in the ego: 'Why do I have my senses?'

This led to the remarkable result that the pupil now felt that everything connected with the senses and with their continuation inwards towards the inner organism was rela-ted to the real environment around him on earth. The senses belong to the winter — that is what the pupil felt. And the whole life through which he was passing, in which the changing winter landscapes corresponded to what he had seen in everyday life, yet which, because they were spiritual, shone for him in great splendour—all these experiences led the pupil to respond in his soul: 'In my Mystery winter experiences, I have passed through aspects of the cosmos that now really belong to the past. The snow and ice of my enchanted winter have shown me what death-dealing forces there are in the cosmos. I now know of the destructive impulses there. And my numbness prior to my mystery winter experiences was the intimation that I was to behold those forces in the cosmos which come over from the past into the present, but in the present are dead cosmic forces.'

This was the realization which the reverberation of his experiences with the male statue conveyed to the pupil.

And now he did not succumb to inner rigidity but to inner heat, a feverish condition of the soul, which began with physical symptoms. It felt like intense pressure inside him, as though everything was under pressure—his breathing and also the blood in his body. He felt extreme anxiety, in fact he was in deep mental distress. And this state brought home to him the second thing he would have to go through. Out of his mental distress there arose in him the realization that he had something within him which his physical nature demanded in his ordinary earthly life. This had to be over-come. His earth ego had to be overcome.

This conviction lived strongly in the pupil's consciousness. Then, when the experience of this inner fever, this mental distress, this feeling that the earthly ego had to be overcome, had lasted for the necessary length of time, something arose in the pupil which he knew was not his previous state of consciousness but a state well known to him, namely, dream consciousness. Whereas from the earlier numbness had come the distinct feeling that he was in a state of consciousness unknown to him in ordinary life, he knew now that his consciousness was a kind of dreaming. He dreamed, but in contrast to what he had dreamt before — although that had been in harmony with what he had experienced — this time he dreamed of the most wonderful summer landscapes. However, now he knew that these were dreams, dreams which filled him with intense joy or intense sadness, depending on whether what came to him from the essence of summer was sad or joyful. But in either case it was accompanied by the intensity of feeling that comes with dreams. You need only remind yourselves of how a dream can affect you. It takes the form of images, but you may wake up from it with a palpitating heart, hot and frightened. The pupil interpreted this intensity of feeling in an elementary and straightforward way, saying to himself: 'My inner being has brought the summer to my consciousness as a dream; the summer has come to me as a dream.'

At the same time the pupil knew that what appeared to his consciousness in a state of continual change, like an enchanted summer, was indicative of impulses leading into the far future of the cosmos. But now he did not feel, as he had previously done, as though he were divided up into his separate senses and multiplied. On the contrary, he now felt himself to be completely gathered together inside himself as an individual being; he felt as though contracted in his heart. And the culmination, the supreme climax of what he was experiencing was this sense of being held together in his heart, this being in full possession of himself and of being inwardly united with the dream of summer — not with the summer as outwardly seen, but with the dream of it. And the pupil said to himself correctly that the future lay in what the dream of summer had revealed and what he had experienced in his own being.

The next experience arising in the pupil was of these two conditions following one another. He was looking into a landscape of meadows and ponds and little lakes for example. Then came a vista of ice and snow which changed into whirling, falling snow, into a mist of falling snowflakes. Then this mist became more and more evanescent, and finally faded into nothingness. And the moment this happened, when he felt himself in empty space, at that moment the summer dreams replaced the winter scenes and he realized in full consciousness that at that point past and future were meeting in his own soul life.

From that point onwards, the pupil had learnt to look at the outer world and to be able to say of it, as of a truth that was to remain with him for all future time: 'In this world which surrounds us, in this world from which we derive our physical nature, something is perpetually dying. And the snow crystals of winter are the outer signs of the spirit that is perpetually dying in matter. As human beings we are not yet capable of feeling completely this dying spirit, which in nature is correctly symbolized in snow and ice, unless initiation has been achieved. But through initiation we know that the spirit is constantly dying in matter, showing it in the process of rigidification in nature. A void is continually being produced. And what is born out of this void is, to begin with, something resembling the dreams of nature. And the dreams of nature contain the seeds for the future of worlds. But the death of worlds and the birth of worlds would not have a meeting-point if the human being were not midway between them.' For if the human being were not there in the middle — as I said, I am simply relating to you the experiences inwardly undergone by the pupils of the Hibernian initiation — if no human being were there between them, the real processes revealed through the new consciousness born of the state of numbness would be an actual death of worlds, with no future to follow. No future would arise to complement the past. Saturn, Sun, Moon and Earth would be there, but no Jupiter, Venus and Vulcan.[26] In order for this cosmic future to unite with the past, the human being had to be there between the past and the future. The pupil knew this simply through what he experienced.

* * *

This sense of a twofold union with the world was an experience which, accompanied by a feeling of inner triumph, came to the pupil as an echo of the experiences connected with the two statues. And the pupil had in this way really learnt on the one hand to expand his soul spiritually into the cosmos and on the other hand to penetrate deeply into a region of his inner being where the forces were not working in the weak way customary in everyday consciousness, but as though they were being stirred to their

very depths by the semi-reality of magical dreams. The pupil
had now learnt to balance this intensity of inner impulses
with the intensity of outer impulses. Out of his relationship
to the winter landscape on the one hand and the summer
landscape on the other, enlightenment had come to him
about external nature and his own self. And he had become
deeply and intimately related to both.

He was then well prepared to go through a kind of
recapitulation. In this recapitulation, his initiation guides put
it very clearly to him: 'While you are experiencing numbness
you must make a deliberate pause, and you must do this
again in the course of going out into cosmic expanses, and for
a third time while you are feeling as though you are being
poured into your senses and multiplied. You must become
inwardly conscious of what each condition is like, and be
able to distinguish clearly between them. You must have an
inner, etheric experience of each of these three conditions.'
And when the pupil, now with full consciousness, called up
again before his soul the state of numbness, there appeared
before him the kind of experience he had had before he came
down to the earth out of spiritual worlds, before the earthly
conception of his body, when he was drawing together out of
the cosmos etheric impulses and forces in order to clothe
himself with an etheric body. In this way the pupil of the
Hibernian Mysteries was brought to experience the final
stage preceding his descent into a physical body.

He had then to become fully aware of the inner experience
of being transported out into the cosmic expanses. This time,
in the recapitulation, he did not feel as though he were being

drawn up by the rays of the sun and the stars, but as though something were coming towards him, as though from all sides the hierarchies were approaching him from the wide expanses, and as though other experiences were also approaching him. And he became aware of circumstances lying farther back in his pre-earthly life. Then he had consciously to recapitulate the experience of being poured out into his senses and dispersed in fragments in the world of the senses. This brought him to the middle point of his existence between death and a new life.

You can see from these remarks that the entry of the initiated person into these hidden worlds — worlds to which humanity, even so, belongs — can happen in the most diverse ways. And from the indications given on many other occasions you will realize, too, that such vision of the super-sensory world was achieved by methods differing widely in the different Mystery centres.[27] In other lectures we shall speak of why it was that such differences were considered appropriate, and why a uniform spiritual path was not adopted in all the mysteries. Today I will merely mention the fact. But the purpose of all these different paths was to unveil the hidden aspects of world and human existence which we have spoken about repeatedly in our present studies as well as in other lectures and writings.

The pupil was then told that he must also recapitulate clearly and learn through his feelings the separate stages of the other conditions he had experienced as after-effects of the other statue, and each condition was to be evoked in consciousness. He carried out these instructions and, in recapitulating the state I described as a kind of soul distress, he had a direct feeling of the after-death experiences in the life of the soul. Then, in his further experiences, he saw a vista of outer nature appearing as a summer landscape, yet as in a dream. As he recapitulated this experience and consciously distinguished it from the other, knowledge came to him of the further course of his life after death. And when he was able to make the experience of contraction really alive and present in his heart, he was able to reach as far as the middle point of existence between death and a new life.

Then the guide of the initiation could say to him:

> Learn, in the spirit, to perceive the winter,
> And you will behold pre-earthly life.
> Learn, in the spirit, to dream the summer,
> And you will experience life after death.

Please note carefully the words I have used, for in the relationship between 'beholding' pre-earthly life and 'experiencing' life after death, and between 'dreaming' and 'perceiving', lies the tremendous difference between the two experiences which the candidate for initiation had in the Mysteries of Hibernia.

The place of this initiation in the whole historic setting of human evolution, its significance in the evolutionary process and the way in which a deeper meaning was indicated when, at the stage of initiation that I described previously, something like a vision of Christ came to the pupil of the Hibernian Mysteries—of these things I shall speak further.

4. Celtic Christianity: The Heritage of the Druids

While the principle of the Mysteries still governed their religious life, the Celts were able to find their way to an understanding of Christianity by inner paths. Christianity came to them not as an alien force, but as a further dimension of their own religious consciousness. The Druids were able to find in it confirmation of things they had already experienced, spiritually, before the historical events were made known to them. Rudolf Steiner has elsewhere described how Christianity itself grew out of the Mysteries once practised in secret in the ancient Near Eastern world and in Greece. Their truths were thereby brought to the knowledge of humanity as a whole. We can also begin to understand how Christianity enabled the Druid wisdom to be given a form for the further development of the Celtic civilization of the West. Rudolf Steiner initiates us into this process, tracing the transformation of the old nature-spirituality into the enduring forms of Celtic Christianity.

Teachings of the Mysteries: the spirit in nature

What we have repeatedly described as the guidance of mankind in the old Druid centres of ritual and religion, in the Mysteries, can be seen arising at a particular period of time coinciding approximately with ancient Iranian and the earliest Mesopotamian culture in the Middle East — it can be seen to coincide with what came from the priests, the great comforters of humankind.[28] Comfort streamed from them and the Mysteries they celebrated; and indeed, human consciousness at that time was greatly in need of comfort. The words of the Mysteries had to contain some quality of soul that could speak to people's hearts with a power of healing and consolation.[29] This is the epoch which exhibited such magnificent creative power (though in a somewhat different form from later periods) in the spheres of art and religion, and a great deal in our art and in our religious ideas derives from that time — particularly the symbols, pictures and ritual ceremonies.

What was the source on which these teachers of the Druid Mysteries drew in order to give such comfort? If the general waking consciousness consisted in the sort of living picture consciousness I have described, there were, nevertheless, at that time too three stages of consciousness. Nowadays we have sleeping, dreaming and waking. In contrast to the waking dream which, as I described earlier, was the normal form of waking consciousness in those days, sleep was not as it is today, when it completely damps down our consciousness. Although with the people of that time, too, consciousness was dimmed during sleep, something of sleep remained on waking. I described it by saying that when people awoke from sleep, they had a sort of after-taste. This was experienced not just on the tongue or in the mouth, but most people felt deeply permeated by certain sweetness of experience which was the after-taste of their sleep. This sweetness which they experienced in sleep spread from their life of sleep into that of waking. This sweetness was to them a test of the healthiness of their life; whereas if other tastes were present it was evidence of illness.

It sounds strange today that an older humanity experienced sweet after-effects of sleep in the limbs, the arms, right down into the finger-tips and the other parts of the body. But the research of the science of the spirit shows that it was so; and the genius of language has retained something of this, though in a crude and materialistic form. A sleeping-draught was once something spiritual, that is, sleep itself, and it was only later that it became an actual liquid draught in a material form. Sleep, then, itself was a draught of nature which extinguished the ordinary memories of day; it was a draught of forgetfulness. Ordinary people only experienced a vague after-feeling but initiation gave the Mystery teachers, who were the leaders of humanity, a more exact consciousness of what really was experienced in sleep. In modern initiation we ascend from our ordinary ideas to spirit-sight, but in those days, while ordinary human beings passed from their dreamlike life into sleep, for which they cultivated a con-sciousness and experienced this after-taste, the mystery priests had the ability to feel their way consciously into sleep and so learned what this after-taste implied. They learned of the flow beyond physical existence, the flow into which the human soul plunged during sleep each night — the flow of the interweaving astral character of the world.

But that was only a second stage beyond the waking and dreaming of ordinary life. The third stage was one of which modern humanity has no knowledge at all, a condition deeper than dreamless sleep today. I have described it as a state of being surrounded by the earth, and this was the condition of human beings at night during deep sleep. Only the priests of the Mysteries could attain consciousness of it by means of their initiation and report on the results of such experiences which constituted the knowledge of those days. Human beings felt themselves embraced by the earth, but they felt something more; they felt that in the ordinary course of the day they had entered a state very near death, a death, however, from which there was an awakening. They experienced this third stage of consciousness as if they had actually descended into the earth and been laid in a grave, but not a grave that could be called an earthly grave. I will try to explain in what follows not only the nature of this grave but how it needs to be understood. When the sun's rays fall on to the earth, they are not merely reflected by the daisies. Farmers know this better than city dwellers, for during the winter they use the sun's warmth which has penetrated into the earth. At that time of the year we have in the earth what has streamed into it during the summer. Not only the sun's warmth but other forces stream into the earth. Yet from the point of view from which I am speaking, this was the less important fact; more important was that the activities of the moon could also penetrate below the surface of the earth to a certain extent. It was a fine, intensely poetical idea of those days—though of course not held as a logical concept as would happen today, but as a picture—that human beings imagined the light of the sun streaming down to earth in the light of the full moon and penetrating a certain distance into the earth, then being reflected not just from the earth's surface but from its interior after the light had been absorbed by the earth.

The silver ebb and flow of the moonlight was experienced by human beings as the rhythmic play of its rays. It was more than just a beautiful picture; the priests of the Mysteries knew something specific about this flowing moonlight. They knew that human beings are subject to gravity as they live on the earth; that gravity holds them to the surface of the earth and that thus the earth draws their being into itself. The forces of the moon were known to work against this force of gravity. They are generally weaker than the vigorous forces of earth's gravity, but they work to counter those forces. It was known that human beings are not just clods of earth captured by the earth's gravity but that they are, rather, in a sort of balance, drawn to the earth by gravity and away from it by the forces of the moon, and that for them as earthly human beings it is the earth which holds the upper hand. But as regards the activity of the head, the effective influence on it is the negative gravity that draws human beings away. Thus though human beings might not be able to fly, at least they could raise their spirits into the stellar spaces. By means of initiation, through the moon activities, humanity in those days learnt from their mystery priests the effect on earthly human beings of their stellar environment.

This was the astrological initiation, so much abused nowadays, which was specially prevalent among the people of ancient Mesopotamia. By its path, human beings could learn not only of the activity of the moon, but also of the sun, Mars, Saturn and so forth. Nowadays human beings — if you will excuse a pictorial way of putting it, for it is hard to describe such things in strictly logical words — have become like worms as far as their knowledge is concerned; not even an earthworm but something worse, a worm for whom it never rains so that it never emerges from the soil! Worms do after all emerge periodically when it rains and then they can enjoy whatever is happening on the surface, and that is healthy for them. With regard to their soul and spirit, modern human beings are worms for whom it never rains, and they are entirely encased in the earth. Thus they believe that the parts of the body grow on earth more or less as stones are formed. They have no idea that the hair on their head is the result of the sun's activity, for they are worms which never come above ground — creatures, that is, which bear the sun forces within them but never come to the surface to investigate them. As the old Mystery priests well knew, human beings have not grown out of the earth like cabbages; they have been created by the joint activity of the whole cosmic environment. You can see, therefore, how human beings in those days felt towards their initiates and leaders of the Mysteries who could tell them on the basis of their training what the cosmic environment signified to human beings.

These priests of the Mysteries could thus proclaim something which I shall have to give in an unimaginative form, since we are not nowadays capable of speaking as they did; they clothed all they said in wonderful poetry. The genius of language made that possible then, but nowadays we can no longer speak in such a way, because language is inadequate. If we had to put into words the message of the priests of the Mysteries to their people who came to them for comfort, feeling themselves thrust into a nature which had lost its spirit, we should have to put it somewhat as follows: 'As long as you remain in your ordinary waking consciousness, your environment will seem to have been robbed of spirit. But if you plunge consciously into the region embraced by the earth, where you can see the power of the star gods in the silvery light of the moon flowing and surging through the earth, you will come to learn—no longer with the previous spontaneity but only by human effort—that external nature is everywhere permeated by spirit beings and bears the gifts of the gods within itself as spirit beings and elemental spirits.'

This was the consolation which the priests of the Mysteries could give their people in ancient days; they made them see that plants are not just beautiful but are permeated by the weaving of the spirit; that the clouds do not just sail through the air but that divine spiritual elemental beings are active in them, and so on. It was towards the spirit of nature that these initiates led the human beings who depended on them for guidance.

Thus at a certain point in human evolution the task of the Mysteries was to make it clear that when nature appeared to have lost the spirit this was only an illusion of ordinary waking consciousness. Actually, spirit was to be found everywhere in nature. There was a time when human beings lived in the spiritual basis of existence and through the Mysteries experienced this spiritual basis even in the sphere which at first sight seemed to have been robbed of spirit. Human beings were still dependent on the spirit in all that affected them, whether instinctively when they had inner spiritual perception or by the Mystery teachings which showed them that nature also was permeated by spirit.

If human evolution had stopped there, our consciousness could never have experienced one of the greatest blessings of humanity, perhaps the very greatest. I mean the experience of free will, of freedom. The old mood of soul, with its instinctively experienced spirituality, had to be damped down. Human beings had to be guided to three other states of consciousness. The feeling of being embraced by the earth, which had enabled the old initiates to attain their star wisdom and their knowledge of nature's spirit, died away completely and the human soul condition came to comprise only dreamless sleep, dreaming and waking. To balance this, there were the beginnings of that sphere of consciousness in which freedom can dawn. What we today call our waking consciousness, which enables us to enjoy our ordinary life and knowledge, was quite unknown to early humanity. Yet through it came the possibility of pure thinking; we may express doubts about its existence, but in it lies the only possible basis for the impulse of freedom. Had human beings never attained such pure thinking — which is actually nothing but pure thinking and does not, as such, guarantee actual reality — they would never have achieved an awareness of freedom.

As humanity developed, human beings' earlier association with the spirit was veiled in darkness; on the other hand, they acquired those three states of consciousness which led them from spiritual heights into the depths of the earth. But out of these depths they found the original forces for the development of freedom. This quality of soul, with its waking, dreaming and sleeping states, had been developing for close on a thousand years and human beings had gone far into that darkness where the light of the spirit does not shine but where the impulse of freedom is to be found. Let us try to understand what human evolution has really been like. There was a time when human beings looked up to the starry heavens and the knowledge they still had of the stars showed them that stellar forces lived within them and that they belonged essentially to the cosmos. But now, human beings — as spiritual beings — were thrust down to earth and the heavens became dark, for the light, though shining down physically from sun or stars, became impenetrable for them. It was as if a curtain had come down, so that they could no longer find any basis for their existence. They could no longer perceive what lay behind the curtain.

We shall see later on how this curtain existed for a thousand years, becoming thicker and thicker, and how this came to expression in the whole mood of human beings. Then a light appeared which did penetrate the curtain and to a certain extent the curtain fell away; it was the light that shone forth on Golgotha. In this way the deed of Golgotha finds its place in human evolution. This deed, accomplished on earth, reopened for human beings the vision of the spiritual element in the world which had once been seen in the wide open spaces of the cosmos. Christ, by passing through the Mystery of Golgotha, brought into human beings' life on earth what had in earlier times been seen in the heavens. The divine spiritual being of Christ descended and lived in a human body so that he might bring this light in a new way to human beings who could no longer leave the earth.

The Great Mysteries: the mystery of Christ

The Hibernian Mysteries belonged to what spiritual science calls the Great Mysteries! For the initiation through which the pupils passed gave them a vista both of pre-earthly life and of life after death. At the same time it gave them a vista of cosmic life, life in which the human being is interwoven and out of which he is born. The pupil was learning to know the microcosm, that is, himself as a being of spirit, soul and body, in connection with the macrocosm. But he also came to know how the macrocosm itself arises, evolves and passes way and undergoes metamorphoses. The Hibernian Mysteries were undoubtedly Great Mysteries.

They were in their prime during the era preceding the Mystery of Golgotha. But the essential feature of these great mysteries was that Christ was spoken of in these Mysteries as a being belonging to the future, just as later on human beings spoke of the Christ as a being who had figured in events of the past. And when, after the first initiation, the image of Christ had been shown to the pupil as he was leaving the temple, the purpose was to bring home to him that the whole evolutionary course of the earth in cosmic existence is orientated to the event of Golgotha, which at that time was presented as an event of the future.

On the island of Hibernia, which later endured so many difficult trials, there was a centre of the Great Mysteries, a centre of 'Christian' Mysteries preceding the event of Golgotha, where the spiritual vision of human beings living prior to that mighty event was directed properly to the Mystery of Golgotha.

And when the Mystery of Golgotha actually occurred, when those remarkable events took place in Palestine which we sum up in the term the Mystery of Golgotha, at that very time solemn festivals were being celebrated within the Hibernian Mysteries and the community associated with them, that is to say, by people who belonged in some way to the Mysteries. And what was actually happening in Palestine was revealed in Hibernia in a hundred different ways in pictures that were not memories of anything in the past. On the island of Hibernia, human beings experienced the Mystery of Golgotha in pictures simultaneously with the historical occurrence in Palestine. When, later on, the Mystery of Golgotha was shown in pictures to people in temples and churches, the pictures were reminders of something that already belonged to the past and which was therefore a historical fact which ordinary consciousness could remember. On the island of Hibernia these pictures were already in existence at a time when they could not have been memories of past history but could only be attained through a spiritual revelation. The events that took place in Palestine at the beginning of our era and were visible there to physical eyes were seen spiritually in Hibernia. On Hibernia, humanity actually experienced the Mystery of Golgotha in the spirit.

And this was the basis of the greatness inherent in everything that subsequently went out from Hibernia into the rest of the civilized world but disappeared as time went on.

I would now ask you to take careful note of the following. Anyone who studies purely external history can find much that is splendid and beautiful, a great deal that is uplifting and enlightening when they look back to the ancient East or to Greece or Rome. Again, they can learn a great deal when it comes, let us say, to the time of Charlemagne and on through the Middle Ages. But just look at how scanty the historical accounts become in the period that begins a few centuries after the birth of Christianity and ends approximately in the ninth or tenth century of the Christian era. If you examine the records that exist, you will find only very few and very meagre accounts of events in those centuries in all the earlier and more honest historical works. It is only after that period that records begin to be more detailed.

Admittedly, later historians feel a certain professional embarrassment at having to deal with the available material so unsatisfactorily. They cannot describe matters of which they have no knowledge and so they think up all kinds of fantastic interpretations which are inserted into the history of those centuries. But it is all so much nonsense. If external history is presented honestly, accounts of the period during which the fall of Rome took place are very meagre. And the same applies to the migrations of peoples, which as a matter of fact were outwardly not nearly so striking as people today suppose but were striking only because of their contrast with the previous and subsequent periods of tranquillity. If you were to calculate today — or rather, if you had calculated in the pre-war period — how many people, let us say, leave Russia for Switzerland every year, you would find that the numbers are greater than they were during the time of the migrations over the same area of Europe. All these things are relative. So that if one were to continue talking in the style adopted when trying to describe the migrations of the peoples, we would have to say that up to the beginning of the war migrations were taking place all over Europe and also across to America. And there was a greater volume of emigration to America than there was in the streams of the migrations of the peoples. But this is not realized. It is nevertheless a fact that records of the period describing the migrations of the peoples and their aftermath are very scanty. Little is known about what was actually happening; little is said, for example, about what was going on in this region or in France or in Germany. But it was precisely in these regions that faint echoes of what had been revealed in the Hibernian mysteries swept over Europe; it was here that the effects and impulses of the great Mysteries of Hibernia penetrated into civilization, even if only in faint echoes.

But then two great streams met. What I am now saying must not be taken as representing any sort of sympathy or antipathy for anything, but merely as describing a historical necessity. Two streams met. The one that came over from the East by way of Greece and Rome depended on the increasingly prevalent faculty connected with the intellect and the senses and worked with what was available as a historical memory of outwardly visible, outwardly experienced events. From Palestine, by way of Greece and Rome, came the tidings of something that had taken place in Palestine in the physical world through Christ, the God, and people received this into their religious life to the extent to which they were capable of understanding it on the basis of a form of consciousness tied to reason and the senses. These tidings spread far and wide, and finally superseded what came over from the West, from Hibernia and, as a last echo of the ancient, instinctive earthly wisdom, took account of the fact that the traditional wisdom of humanity was now shedding its light into a new kind of consciousness. From Hibernia there spread across Europe an impulse which in the matter of spiritual illumination did not depend upon physical vision or 'proof' based upon evidence of any actual historical event. This impulse spread in the form of Hibernian religious ceremonies and wisdom. It was concerned with illumination that comes to human beings from the spiritual world in the case of an event which, like the Mystery of Golgotha, had taken place simultaneously in physical reality in another part of the world. In Hibernia the physical reality of the event in Palestine was seen spiritually.

But the mentality that could grasp only physical reality overshadowed the impulse that relied upon the spiritual upliftment and deepening of the life of the soul. And gradually, because of the inevitable necessity of which we have spoken with regard to other aspects, the impulse connected principally with physical existence gained the upper hand over the impulse associated with spiritual vision. The tidings of the Redeemer present in a physical body on earth obscured the wonderful imaginations coming over from Hibernia which could be presented in cult and ritual — those magnificent imaginations portraying the Redeemer as a spiritual being which took no account, either in the corresponding rituals or descriptions, of the fact that what had come to pass was also a physical event. Still less could this latter aspect be taken into account before the actual event by cults which had been instituted in the pre-Christian era.

And the time came when human beings became steadily immune to everything that was not physically perceptible, when they came to the point of no longer accepting as truth anything that was not physically perceptible. Thus the substance of the wisdom coming over from Hibernia was no longer understood; nor was the art which came from there felt to be an expression of cosmic truth. The consequence was the ever-increasing growth of a science that was not a Hibernian science but one concerned only with what the senses perceive, and also of a form of art that was not Hibernian art.

What humanity once experienced actually did remain alive in the subconscious. It only dried up altogether in the early period of the Thirty Years' War. In the first half of the seventeenth century there was an influx of what had once been great, impressive spiritual truth. The mystics alone preserved its impression in their souls, but the real substance, the spiritual substance, was totally lost. It was the time for reason to be victorious and to prepare the epoch of freedom.

And today we look back at these things and find our gaze directed with a very great and deep interest to the Hibernian Mysteries, for they are truly the last Great Mysteries through which the secrets of human and cosmic life could be revealed. Today, when we delve into them again, we realize for the first time how great these Hibernian mysteries were. But our vision cannot really penetrate into their depths if we have not first fathomed them through our own independent efforts. And even when this has been achieved, a strange thing happens.

When one approaches the pictures of the Hibernian mysteries in the Akashic Record,[30] one feels that something is repelling one. It is as though some force were holding one back, as though one's soul could not reach them. The nearer one approaches, the more one's goal seems to be eclipsed, and a kind of bewilderment comes over one's soul. One has to work one's way through this bewilderment, and the only possible way of doing so is to rekindle one's own independently acquired knowledge of similar matters. And then one understands why it is so difficult to approach the Hibernian Mysteries. It becomes evident that they were the final echo of an ancient gift to humanity from the divine spiritual powers, but that when these Mysteries withdrew into a shadowy existence, they were at the same time surrounded by a strong defence so that human beings cannot find their way to them if they maintain a passive attitude of soul. They can approach these Mysteries only by kindling their own spiritual activity – in other words, by becoming modern human beings in the true sense.

Access to the Hibernian Mysteries was barred so that people could not approach them passively but must experience with the full activity of consciousness that which must be discovered inwardly in this age of freedom. Neither by the study of history nor by clairvoyant vision of great and wonderful ancient secrets can these mysteries be discovered, but only by the exercise of a human being's own conscious, inner activity.

The Great Mysteries of Hibernia thus provide the very strongest indication of the fact that a new age began at the time when they faded into the realm of shadows. But they can be seen again today in all their glory and majesty by a soul sustained by inner freedom. For through true inner activity they can indeed be seen again when the opposing forces, with their menace of bewilderment, are overcome and the way is opened to a vision of the revelations that were once accessible to those who were to be initiated — revelations of the ancient secrets of the spiritual wisdom, instinctive it is true but none the less sublime, that were once dispensed to earthly humanity as a primal power of the soul. The most beautiful and significant memorials in later times to the primal wisdom of humanity, the sublime grace of divine spiritual beings evident in the earliest stages of humanity, the most beautiful soul and spiritual tokens of that age are the pictures that can be revealed to us when we direct our spiritual gaze to the Mysteries of Hibernia.

Appendix: The Function of the Standing Stones

Only through the science of the spirit of today can we arrive again at the true form in which things were perceived in ancient times. People who want to shut out modern spiritual science have no means of understanding the language spoken by those who possessed the primeval wisdom of humankind; hence they are fundamentally unable to picture things historically. Those who know nothing of the spiritual world are often quite naive in the way they expound and interpret the old records of primeval peoples. Thus we find in documents which perhaps contain primeval wisdom now obscured such wonderful phrases as 'the wheel of births'.[31] These phrases must be understood by rediscovering the reality to which they allude. People who want to give a picture of the true history of humankind on earth must therefore not shrink from first learning to know the meaning of the language used in those far-off days.

I might very well have begun by picturing the historical evolution of mankind in the terms used in the ancient records; but then you would not have heard words used merely as words, as they so often are in the world today. Hence, if one is to give a true picture of that part of reality lived through by a man during a historical period, one has to start by describing his relationship to the spiritual worlds. For only in this way are we enabled to find our way about in the language used, and in all that was done in those ancient times to maintain a connection with the spiritual worlds. I have described how the Druid priests set up stones and screened them in such a way that by gazing into the shadow thrown within this structure and looking through the stones they could gain information concerning the will of the spiritual worlds which left an impression at the physical level. But something else was also connected with this. In the spiritual world there is not only a departure but also always a return. Just as there are forces of time which carry us forward through physical existence on earth and after death draw us backwards again, so there are forces in the structures set up by the Druids which descend from above and also forces which ascend from below. Hence the Druid priests watched both a downward and an upward stream in these structures. When their structures were set up on appropriate sites, the priests could perceive not only the will of divine spirits coming down from the cosmos but, because in the upward stream the one-dimensional element prevailed,[32] they could perceive the good or bad elements that belonged to members of their community and flowed out from them into the cosmos. Thus these stones served as an observatory for the Druid priests, enabling them to see how the souls of their people stood in relation to the cosmos.

All these secrets, all these Mysteries, are connected with things that have been left over from ancient times and exist now in such a decadent form. They can be understood only when through the power of individual imagination, inspiration and intuition the world of the spirit is raised once more out of its hidden existence and brought into consciousness.

Notes

1 John Matthews, *The Druid Sourcebook* (London 1997).
2 Cf. Frank Teichmann, *Der Mensch und sein Tempel* (Stuttgart 1999).
3 *Gallic Wars*, VI, 13–14.
4 See pp. 22–3, 32–6.
5 See pp. 10–14.
6 A good account of the Penmaenmawr Conference of August 1923 and its place in the development of anthroposophy is given by T.H. Meyer, *D.N. Dunlop* (London 1992), pp. 146ff. Rudolf Steiner made it the occasion, indeed, for reaffirming the central spiritual truths that were already being applied in a great variety of projects and spheres of work at that time, drawing them together around the 'core' of anthroposophy.
7 Steiner, *The Apocalypse of John* (London 1977). Introductory Lecture.
8 The description is given in Gerald of Wales, *Description of Ireland*. For discussion see J. Sharkey, *Celtic Mysteries* (London 1975), p. 13.
9 Piggott, *The Druids* (Harmondsworth 1974), p. 30.
10 Below, p. 27.
11 Rex Raab, *Eloquent Concrete* (London 1979); H. Biesantz and A. Klingborg, *The Goetheanum* (London 1979).
12 The lectures which Rudolf Steiner gave there in August 1923 are published as *The Evolution of Consciousness* (London 1966).
13 See 'Excursus', on pp. 25–6.
14 Stuttgart, in southern Germany.

15 The sculptured wooden building at Dornach had been erected as the 'spiritual home' of the Anthroposophical Society according to architectural designs by Rudolf Steiner — see further his lectures *Architecture as a Synthesis of the Arts* (London 1999). It was burned down, probably by the hand of an arsonist, on New Year's Night 1922–3. Subsequently Rudolf Steiner drew up plans for the 'Second Goetheanum', in flowing forms cast in concrete, which now stands on the same site. See further Rex Raab et al., *Eloquent Concrete* (London 1979). The Goetheanum houses the Anthroposophical Society, and serves as the setting for festivals, conferences, lectures, concerts, etc. related to Rudolf Steiner's work.

16 Eurythmy is an art of movement developed by Rudolf and Marie Steiner, which can be described as 'visible speech' or 'visible music'. See further M. Lundgren et al., *Eurythmy and the Impulse of Dance* (London 1974).

17 On Loki, the 'Lucifer' of Norse mythology, cf. the remarks of Rudolf Steiner, *The Mission of Folk-souls* (London 1970), pp. 141ff.

18 The place of the Penmaenmawr Conference in the history of the movement is well brought out by Thomas Meyer, *D. N. Dunlop* (London 1992), pp. 46ff.

19 On Odin and his mastery of the runes, see further Rudolf Steiner, *The Mission of Folk-souls*, pp. 133ff.

20 Sun and Moon here denote former stages of cosmic evolution, of which the presently existing sun and moon are a kind of physical remnant. Steiner describes a primal planet which contains spiritually all that will unfold in our solar system ('ancient Saturn'); after the Sun and Moon stages, there follows the emergence of the physical Earth. Others among the present planets are a kind of anticipation of future spiritual-cosmic

states. The whole sequence of cosmic evolution can therefore be summed up in the terms: Saturn; Sun; Moon; Earth; Jupiter; Venus; Vulcan. See the lengthy account of cosmic evolution in Steiner, *Occult Science* (London 1969), pp. 102–221 (also available as *An Outline of Esoteric Science*, New York 1997). Ancient cosmologies and religions often reflect knowledge of these cosmic relationships from the standpoint of the ancient instinctive clairvoyance.

21 'That which springs out of the body of the earth,' says Steiner (in contrast to what comes down from the cosmos into earthly life), 'is described in Norse mythology as belonging to the realm of the giants.' Steiner, *The Mission of Folk-souls*, p. 171.

22 See further *The Mission of Folk-souls*, pp. 148ff.

23 Scene 7 in Steiner's play *The Portal of Initiation* involves the characters' recollection of a previous life in ancient Ireland. Hibernia is the Roman name for Ireland.

24 In modern times not only do we tend to relate only to the results of sense experience at the expense of the spirit, we also have a blinkered understanding of the 'five senses'. In reality our range of sensory experience is already much wider than this. Phenomenologically, twelve different domains of experience, some of them more inward (sense of movement, sense of equilibrium, etc.), some of them more external, have the character of direct perception of sense-qualities. See Rudolf Steiner, *Man as a Being of Sense and Perception* (Vancouver 1981).

25 Ensoulment by such higher beings was experienced frequently by very ancient humanity, and even to some extent later through the mysteries. 'In post-Atlantean times,' comments Steiner, 'the great leaders of humanity were ensouled by angelic beings who had descended into their physical, etheric and astral bodies. The mighty leaders of the first post-Atlantean

periods did not have only human physical, etheric and astral bodies; each leader was permeated by an angel.' Steiner, *The Spiritual Hierarchies* (New York 1970).

26 On the meaning of this cosmic sequence, see note 20 above.

27 See further Steiner, *Mystery Knowledge and Mystery Centres* (London 1997).

28 That is around 3000 BC.

29 On the nature of this 'consolation', cf. Steiner's remarks in *Building Stones for an Understanding of the Mystery of Golgotha* (London 1972), pp. 42ff (esp. p. 47).

30 'If we are able to raise our faculty of perception and look through the visible world to the invisible, we arrive at length at a point where we have before us what may be called a mighty spiritual panorama wherein all the past events of the world are displayed. These abiding traces of all spiritual happenings may be termed the "Akashic Records"': Steiner, *Occult Science* (London 1969), p. 105. Rudolf Steiner constantly emphasized the difficulty of obtaining accurate results from the reading of the Akashic Records, requiring a high level of clairvoyance.

31 The phrase is taken from the *Bhagavadgita*. See further Steiner, *The Evolution of Consciousness*, pp. 134ff.

32 See the comments by Rudolf Steiner on the two-dimensional character of imaginative experience (above, pp. 25–6). The one-dimensionality of inspiration, as Steiner calls the next higher level of spiritual experience, betokens a closer link to what is experienced. In the still higher stage of intuition, we are united directly with the essence of a thing or being. Cf. Steiner, *Evolution of Consciousness*, pp. 29ff.

Sources

This book comprises thematic extracts from the work of Rudolf Steiner.

'The Druids at Penmaenmawr' reproduces Steiner, *Man in the Past, Present and the Future. The Sun Initiation of the Druid Priest and his Moon Science* (London 1966), pp. 17–27 (translated from GA 228 in the edition of Steiner's original works).

'Excursus: Spiritual imaginations' reproduces a passage from Rudolf Steiner, *The Evolution of Consciousness* (London 1991), pp. 27–8 (translated from GA 227 in the edition of Steiner's work).

'The Sun Initiation of the Druid Priests' reproduces *Man in the Past, Present and the Future*, pp. 66–77.

'The Mysteries of ancient Ireland' reproduces Steiner, *Mystery Knowledge and Mystery Centres* (London 1997), pp. 117–21; 130–35; and 138–40 (translated from GA 232 in the edition of Steiner's original work).

'Teachings of the Mysteries' reproduces *Man in the Past, Present and the Future*, pp. 32–9.

'The Great Mysteries: The mystery of Christ' reproduces Steiner, *Mystery Knowledge and Mystery Centres*, pp. 151–60.

The 'Appendix' reproduces Steiner, *The Evolution of Consciousness*, pp. 133–4.

Suggested Further Reading

By Rudolf Steiner

Ancient Myths and the New Isis Mystery (New York 1997)

Building Stones for an Understanding of the Mystery of Golgotha (London 1972)

Christianity as Mystical Fact (New York 1997)

The Evolution of Consciousness (London 1991)

Man in the Past, Present and the Future. The Sun-Initiation of the Druid Priest and his Moon Science (London 1966)

The Mission of Folk-souls (London 1970)

Mysteries of the East and Christianity (London 1972)

Mystery Knowledge and Mystery Centres (London 1997)

Occult Science (London 1969). Also available as *An Outline of Esoteric Science* (New York 1997)

World History and the Mysteries (London 1997)

Note Regarding Rudolf Steiner's Lectures

The lectures and addresses contained in this volume have been translated from the German, which is based on stenographic and other recorded texts that were in most cases never seen or revised by the lecturer. Hence, due to human errors in hearing and transcription, they may contain mistakes and faulty passages. Every effort has been made to ensure that this is not the case. Some of the lectures were given to audiences more familiar with anthroposophy; these are the so-called 'private' or 'members' lectures. Other lectures, like the written works, were intended for the general public. The difference between these, as Rudolf Steiner indicates in his *Autobiography*, is twofold. On the one hand, the members' lectures take for granted a background in and commitment to anthroposophy; in the public lectures this was not the case. At the same time, the members' lectures address the concerns and dilemmas of the members, while the public work speaks directly out of Steiner's own understanding of universal needs. Nevertheless, as Rudolf Steiner stresses: 'Nothing was ever said that was not solely the result of my direct experience of the growing content of anthroposophy. There was never any question of concessions to the prejudices and preferences of the members. Whoever reads these privately printed lectures can take them to represent anthroposophy in the fullest sense. Thus it was possible without hesitation—when the complaints in this direction became too persistent—to depart from the custom of circulating this material "For members only". But it must be borne in mind that faulty passages do occur in these reports not revised by myself.' Earlier in the same chapter, he states: 'Had I been able to correct them [the private lectures], the restriction *for members only* would have been unnecessary from the beginning.'

The original German editions on which this text is based were published by Rudolf Steiner Verlag, Dornach, Switzerland in the collected edition (*Gesamtausgabe*, 'GA') of Rudolf Steiner's work. All publications are edited by the Rudolf Steiner Nachlassverwaltung (estate), which wholly owns both Rudolf Steiner Verlag and the Rudolf Steiner Archive. The organization relies solely on donations to continue its activity.

For further information please contact:

Rudolf Steiner Archiv
Postfach 135
CH-4143 Dornach

or:

www.rudolf-steiner.com

ALSO AVAILABLE IN THE 'POCKET
LIBRARY OF SPIRITUAL WISDOM' SERIES

Rudolf Steiner
Alchemy
The Evolution of the Mysteries

Alchemy and the Rise of the Modern Mysteries; The Loss of
the Divine and the Alchemical Quest; Mysteries of the
Metals; The Standpoint of Human Wisdom Today; Alchemy
and Consciousness — the Transformation; Alchemy and
Archangels; The Alchemy of Nature — Mercury, Sulphur,
Salt; Beyond Nature Consciousness — the Spiritual Goal.

RSP; 112pp; 17 × 12 cm; 1 85584 089 8; pb; £7.95

Rudolf Steiner
Atlantis
The Fate of a Lost Land and its Secret Knowledge

The Continent of Atlantis; The Moving Continents; The
History of Atlantis; The Earliest Civilizations; The
Beginnings of Thought; Etheric Technology — Atlantean
'Magic' Powers; Twilight of the Magicians; The Divine
Messengers; Atlantean Secret Knowledge — it's Betrayal and
Subsequent Fate; The Origins of the Mysteries; Atlantis and
Spiritual Evolution

RSP; 112pp; 17 × 12 cm; 1 85584 079 0; pb; £7.95

Rudolf Steiner
Christian Rosenkreutz
The Mystery, Teaching and Mission of a Master

The Mystery of Christian Rosenkreutz; The Working of
Christian Rosenkreutz Today and in the Past; Christian
Rosenkreutz as the Guardian of Modern Knowledge; From
Ancient to Modern in Rosicrucian Teachings; Christian
Rosenkreutz at the 'Chymical Wedding'; The Cosmic
Mission of Christian Rosenkreutz; The Question of
'Rosicrucian' Literature.

RSP; 96pp; 17 × 12 cm; 1 85584 084 7; pb; £7.95

Rudolf Steiner
The Goddess
From Natura to the Divine Sophia

Rediscovering the Goddess Natura; Retracing our Steps—
Mediaeval Thought and the School of Chartres; The Goddess
Natura in the Ancient Mysteries; The Goddess in the
Beginning—the Birth of the Word; Esoteric Christianity—the
Virgin Sophia; the Search for the New Isis; The Renewal of
the Mysteries; The Modern Isis, the Divine Sophia.

RSP; 112pp; 17 × 12 cm; 1 85584 094 4; pb; £7.95

Rudolf Steiner
The Holy Grail
The Quest for the Renewal of the Mysteries

From the Mysteries to Christianity; Death and Resurrection
in Ancient Egypt—the Miracle of Initiation; The Mystery of
Golgotha; The Mystery of the Higher Ego—the Holy Grail;
The Grail and the Spiritual Evolution of Humanity; The
Gnostic Crisis and the Loss of the Mysteries; Stages of
Evolution—Archaic Clairvoyance; The Role of the Mysteries;
The Secret of Evolution—the Holy Grail.

RSP; 96pp; 17 × 12 cm; 1 85584 074 X; pb; £7.95